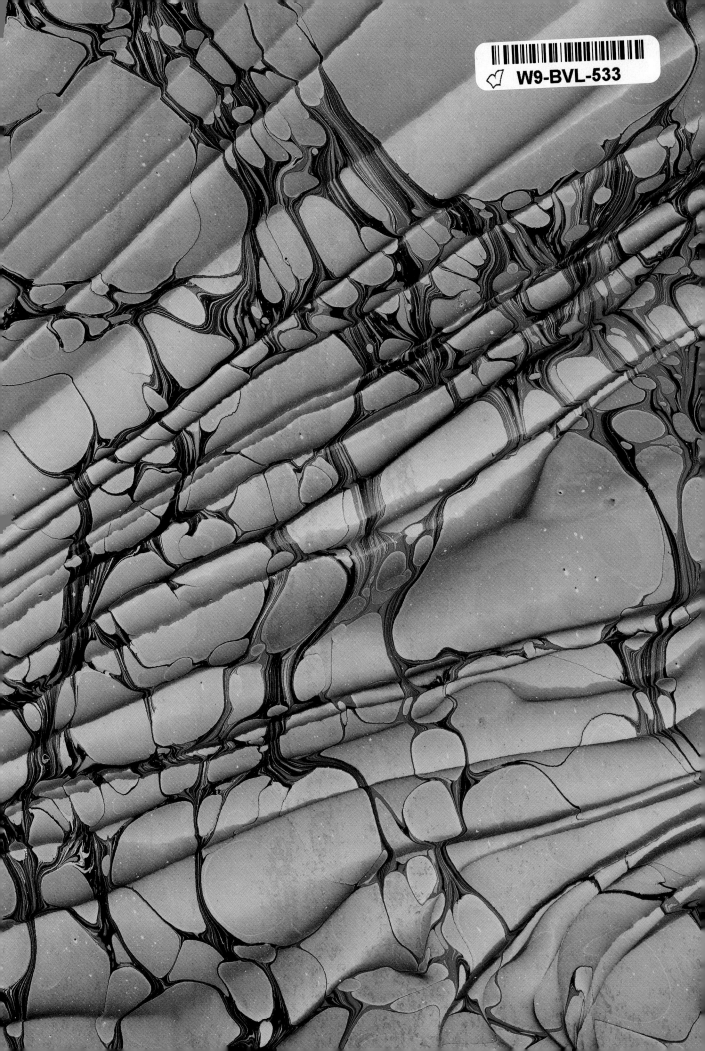

1998

Sue + Randy,

We wish you
a very Merry Christmas.

Gil + Dee

P.S. Thanks for all the fun
"Bridge" memories!

Pictures in the Fire

Text by Williston Fish
Compiled by Harold Darling

Blue Lantern Books
1997

Blue Lantern Books
PO Box 4399 • Seattle • Washington
98104

Foreword

He was stronger and cleverer, no doubt, than other men, and in many broad lines of business he had grown rich, until his wealth exceeded exaggeration. One morning, in his office, he directed a request to his confidential lawyer to come to him in the afternoon — he intended to have his will drawn. A will is a solemn matter, even with men whose life is given up to business, and who are by habit mindful of their future. After giving this direction he took up no other matter, but sat at his desk alone and in silence.

It was a day when summer was first new. The pale leaves upon the trees were starting forth upon the yet unbending branches. The grass in the parks had a freshness in its green like the freshness of the blue in the sky and of the yellow of the sun — a freshness to make one wish that life might renew its youth. The clear breezes from the south wantoned about, and then were still, as if loath to go finally away. Half idly, half thoughtfully, the rich man wrote upon the white paper before him, beginning what he wrote with capital letters, such as he had not made since, as a boy in school, he had taken pride in his skill with the pen:

I Charles Lounsbury, being of sound mind and disposing memory, do hereby make and publish this, my last will and testament, in order as justly as may be to distribute my interest in the world among succeeding men.

 give to good fathers and mothers, in trust for their children, all good little words of praise and encouragement, and all quaint little pet names and endearments, and I charge said parents to use them justly and generously, as the needs of their children may require.

I leave to children inclusively, but only for the term of their childhood, all and every, the flowers of the fields, and the blossoms of the woods, with the right to play among them freely according to the customs of children, warning them at the same time against thistles and thorns.

 nd I devise to children the banks of the brooks, the golden sands beneath the waters thereof, the odors of the willows that dip therein, and the white clouds that float high over the giant trees.

nd I leave
the children the long, long days to be
merry in, in a thousand ways,

*and the night
and the moon
and the train
of the milky
way to
wonder at,
but subject
nevertheless
to the rights
hereinafter given to lovers.*

 devise to young people jointly all the useful idle fields and commons where ball may be played;

*all pleasant
waters where one
may swim;*

all snow-clad hills

where one may coast;

and all streams and ponds where one may fish, or where, when grim winter comes, one may skate;

to have and to hold the same for the period of their youth,

and all meadows with the clover blos-
soms and butterflies thereof, the
woods and their appurtenances, the
squirrels and birds, and echoes and
strange noises, and all distant places
which may be visited, together with
the adventures there found.

nd I give to each his own place at the fireside at night, with all pictures that may be seen in the burning wood, to enjoy without let or hindrance and without any incumbrance or care.

o lovers, I devise their imaginary world with what-ever they may need– as the stars of the sky, the red roses by the wall, the bloom of the hawthorn, the sweet strains of music, and aught else they may desire to figure to each other the lastingness and beauty of their love.

o young men jointly, I devise and bequeath all boisterous, inspiring sports of rivalry, and I give to them the disdain of weakness and undaunted confidence in their own strength, though they are rude.

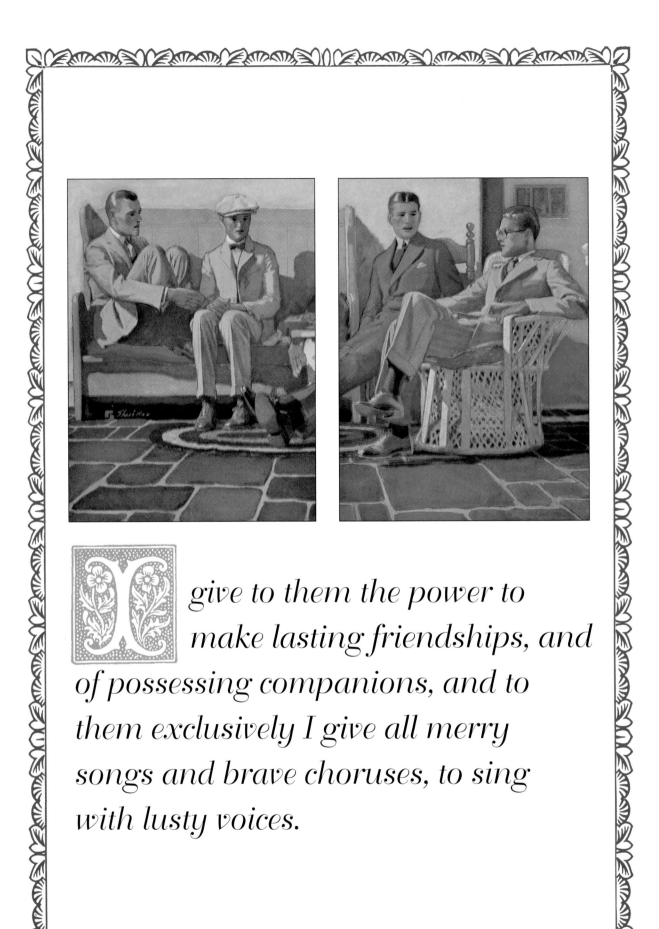

I give to them the power to make lasting friendships, and of possessing companions, and to them exclusively I give all merry songs and brave choruses, to sing with lusty voices.

 nd to those who are no longer children or youths or lovers, I leave memory.

 nd I bequeath to them the volumes of poems of Burns and Shakespeare and of other poets, if there be others, to the end that they may live over the old days again, freely and fully, without tithe or diminution.

 o our loved ones with snowy crowns I bequeath the happiness of old age, the love and gratitude of their children until they fall asleep.

This book was designed and set in Bellvue by
The Blue Lantern Studio.

Picture Credits

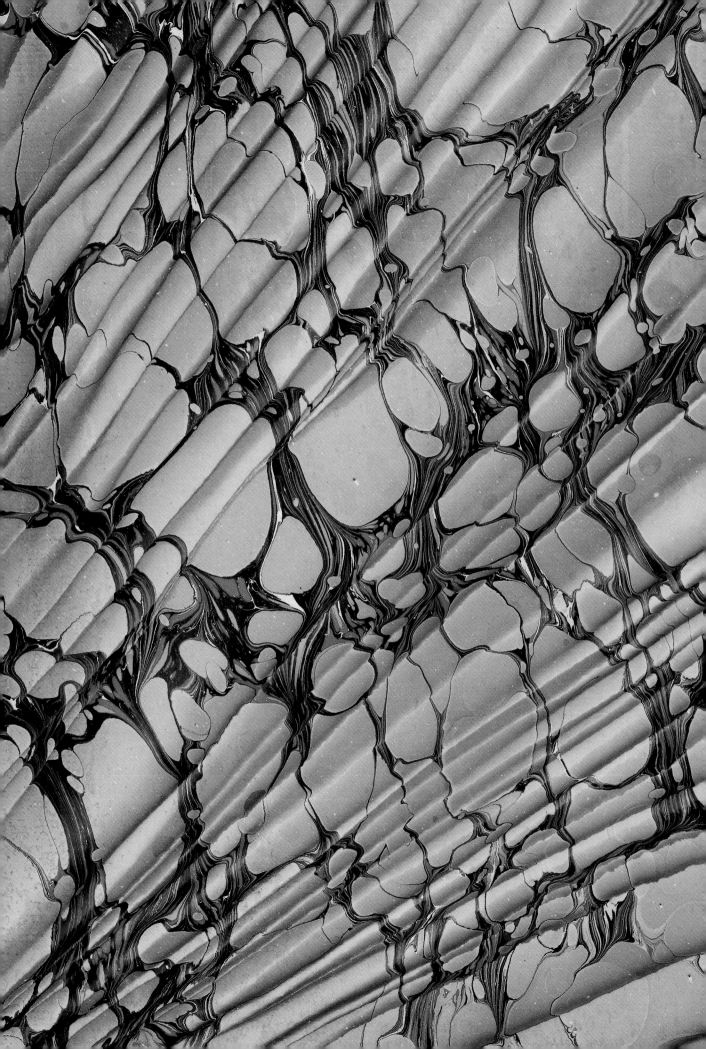